Contents

Some words are shown in bold, **like this**. You can find out what they mean by looking in the glossary.

What are rivers?

Rivers are channels of fresh water flowing through the landscape. The start of a river is called its **source**. The river flows from its source downhill towards the sea.

A river grows bigger as it travels towards the sea. Small rivers and **streams** join together and form bigger rivers. Rivers bring water to the land so that plants can grow. People use rivers and water in lots of ways. The United Kingdom has many important rivers.

This river is flowing fast as it travels downhill from its source.

Great Rivers

Rivers of the United Kingdom

Catherine Brereton

Raintree is an imprint of Capstone Global Library Limited, a company incorporated in England and Wales having its registered office at 264 Banbury Road, Oxford, OX2 7DY – Registered company number 6695582

www.raintree.co.uk
myorders@raintree.co.uk

Produced by Brown Bear Books Ltd:
Text: Catherine Brereton
Design Manager: Keith Davis
Editorial Director: Lindsey Lowe
Children's Publisher: Anne O'Daly
Picture Manager: Sophie Mortimer
Printed and bound in India

ISBN: 978 1 4747 5400 2   ISBN: 978 1 4747 5404 0
21 20 19 18 17   22 21 20 19 18
10 9 8 7 6 5 3 2 1   10 9 8 7 6 5 3 2 1

British Library Cataloguing-in-Publication Data
A full catalogue record for this book is available from the British Library.

Acknowledgements
We would like to thank the following for permission to reproduce photographs:
123rf: Peter Titmuss, 15; Alamy: Acorn 5, 22, Commission Air, 7, Epicscotland, 25, Heather Drake, 21, i4images rm, 9, Mike Howitt, 23, Powered by Light/Alan Spencer, 8; Braintree Canoeing Club: 14; iStock: 1, 28 (centre left), CaronB, 5 (top), George-Standen, 11, John F. Scott, 28 (right), Jolanda Aalbers, 5 (bottom), MikeLane45, 13; Public Domain: FT magazine, 19; Roger Keech Productions Ltd: 27; Shutterstock: Helen Hotson, 4-5, IR Stone, 18, Madrugada Verde, cover, Martin Prochazkacz, 26, Maziarz, 17; Thinkstock: iStock, 28 (bottom)

Brown Bear Books has made every attempt to contact copyright holders of material reproduced in this book. Any omissions will be rectified in subsequent printings if notice is given to the publisher. If anyone has any information please contact licensing@brownbearbooks.co.uk

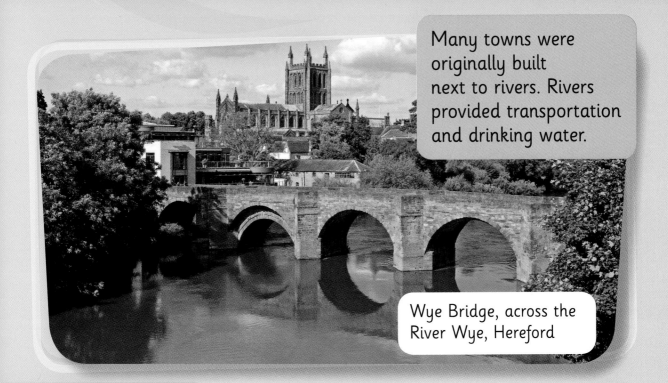

Many towns were originally built next to rivers. Rivers provided transportation and drinking water.

Wye Bridge, across the River Wye, Hereford

Golitha Falls, Cornwall

Rivers are home to many types of birds, insects, fish and other animals.

The Avon

The River Avon begins at a **spring** in central England. There are ten British rivers called Avon. This one is sometimes called the Warwickshire Avon or the Upper Avon.

Where:
Central England

How long: 154 km (96 miles)

Main towns/cities: Rugby, Warwick, Stratford-upon-Avon, Evesham, Tewkesbury

The Avon is also a **tributary** of the River Severn. It joins the Severn at Tewkesbury.

Rugby

Warwick

Stratford-upon-Avon

Tewkesbury

Evesham

— *River Severn*

Bristol Channel

The river gets wider and deeper as it flows along.

As it goes along, the River Avon shapes the landscape. It flows along in big curves called meanders. The river flows through a **valley**. The Avon valley is famous for its stunning scenery.

Rivers and **canals** were once important for transporting goods. **Locks** were built to raise or lower boats where stretches of the river or canal were at different levels. Now the boats on the River Avon are mainly for fun.

Narrowboats have to go through 17 locks on the Avon.

Boats gather each year to celebrate the river festival in Stratford-upon-Avon.

One of Britain's most famous writers, William Shakespeare, was born in Stratford-upon-Avon. The town is popular with tourists. Many people visit the town to see Shakespeare's plays performed at The Royal Shakespeare Theatre next to the river.

The Mersey

The River Mersey begins in the Pennine Hills. It becomes a wide **estuary** before it meets the sea in Liverpool Bay. **Ferries** have taken people across the Mersey estuary since **medieval** times.

The Mersey was once very dirty. It has been cleaned up and wildlife, such as otters and even seals, now live there again.

Where: North-west England

How long: 110 km (70 miles)

Main towns/cities: Stockport, Warrington, Birkenhead, Liverpool

Irish Sea

Liverpool

Birkenhead

Warrington

Stockport

The old Albert Dock in Liverpool is now a tourist attraction. Museums tell the story of the city's past.

Liverpool is a busy **port**. Until the mid-1900s ships carried sugar, cotton, timber and grain all over the world. Today, Liverpool is an important port for huge container ships.

The Severn

The River Severn is the longest river in the United Kingdom. It starts at the top of the Cambrian Mountains in Wales. The river flows down through Wales and England to the Bristol Channel.

The **estuary** of the River Severn is over 8 km (5 miles) wide.

Where: Wales and West of England

How long: 354 km (220 miles)

Main towns/cities: Newtown, Welshpool, Shrewsbury, Ironbridge, Worcester, Gloucester

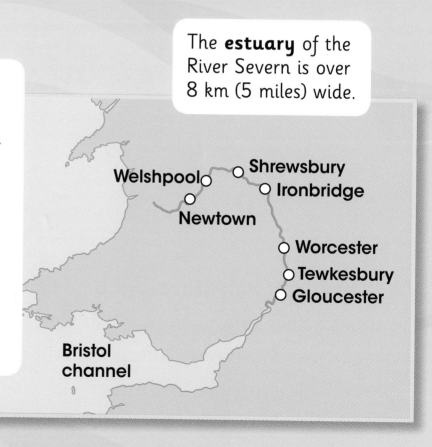

Welshpool
Shrewsbury
Ironbridge
Newtown
Worcester
Tewkesbury
Gloucester
Bristol channel

This brightly-coloured kingfisher dives into the water of the River Severn to catch a fish.

Rivers are important **habitats** for animals.
Fish, frogs, newts and snails live in rivers.
The River Severn is home to many animals.
Dragonflies flutter above the water. Birds hunt
for food in the river and nest on its banks.

In some rivers, the **tide** coming in from the sea travels all the way up the river. This is called a tidal bore. The River Severn has one of the largest tidal bores in the world! There are 260 tidal bores on the Severn each year.

A tidal bore makes waves as high as 3 metres (10 feet).

The bridge at Ironbridge was built in 1779.

The **Industrial Revolution** started in the Severn **valley** in the 1770s. Abraham Darby invented a new way to make iron and built the world's first cast-iron bridge. The bridge spans the River Severn.

The Thames

London is the **capital city** of the United Kingdom. The River Thames flows through central London. More than eight million people live in London. Some people use river buses and taxis to get to and from work.

Two thirds of London's drinking water comes from the River Thames.

Where:
South-east England

How long: 330 km (205 miles)

Main towns/cities:
Oxford, Reading, Henley, Marlow, Windsor, Teddington, London, Southend-on-Sea

Oxford

Henley

Marlow

Southend-on-Sea

Reading

Windsor

LONDON

Teddington

Tower Bridge is London's most famous bridge across the Thames.

The River Thames flows east from a small **stream** in the Cotswold Hills. It opens into a wide **estuary** at Southend-on-Sea. A footpath, the Thames Path National Trail, starts in the Cotswold Hills. It ends at the Thames Barrier in Greenwich, London.

If there is a storm or a very high **tide**, London is at risk of being flooded. The Thames Barrier protects the city. If there is going to be a high tide, the gates are shut to keep the water out.

The Thames Barrier has ten huge steel gates across the river.

The Thames froze solid for two months in 1683–1684. Londoners set up camps selling food and drink.

Between 1600 and 1814 winter frost fairs were held on the River Thames. The water froze solid. Winters are warmer now. The river no longer freezes but people still have fun on the Thames. Today, they enjoy water sports such as rowing and kayaking.

The Trent

The River Trent is the third-longest river in the United Kingdom. Its **source** is at Biddulph Moor in Staffordshire. It flows from there through the Midlands and into the Humber **estuary**.

The River Trent flows northwards, which is unusual for rivers in Britain.

Where: Central England

How long: 270 km (168 miles)

Main towns/cities: Stoke-on-Trent, Burton-upon-Trent, Nottingham, Newark

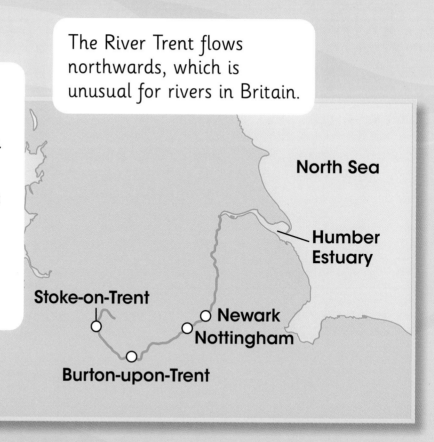

North Sea

Humber Estuary

Stoke-on-Trent

Newark
Nottingham

Burton-upon-Trent

Trent Bridge in Nottingham is one of the Trent's most famous landmarks.

Nottingham first had a bridge and a busy market in **medieval** times. The town grew quickly as the river became an important route for transport and **trade**.

Fast-flowing water from rivers creates energy.
People can use the energy to drive **turbines**
in machines called **generators**. These machines
create electricity.

Beeston Weir is one of many
small power stations along
the River Trent.

Rubbish in the River Trent is one type of pollution. It can harm wildlife.

Pollution is a problem in many rivers. Harmful chemicals from factories and farms sometimes spill into rivers. Sewage can also be a problem. Pollution kills fish and other wildlife. It is also dangerous for people. It is important to keep rivers clean.

The Tweed

The River Tweed starts as a tiny **burn** at Tweed's Well, high in the Scottish mountains. The river journeys through southern Scotland. It crosses the border into England and flows into the North Sea.

For 27 km (17 miles) the River Tweed forms the border between Scotland and England.

Where: Scotland and North of England

How long: 156 km (97 miles)

Main towns/cities: Peebles, Galashiels, Kelso, Berwick-upon-Tweed

North Sea

Berwick-upon-Tweed

Peebles

Kelso

Galashiels

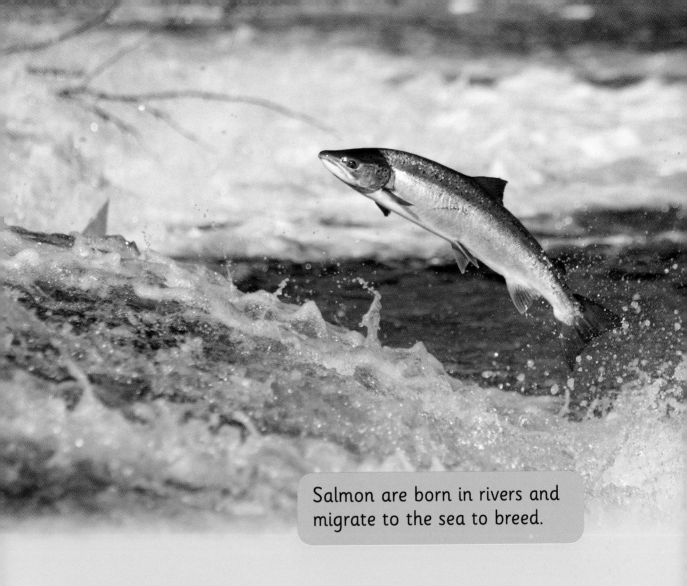

Salmon are born in rivers and migrate to the sea to breed.

The Tweed is famous for its salmon. The clean, cold waters make it an ideal **habitat** for these fish. Many people visit the Tweed to go salmon fishing. They also visit the area to spot the rare osprey. Ospreys are birds of prey that feed on salmon.

A hundred years ago, ospreys had disappeared from Britain. They were killed by **pesticides** used on farms, and people stole their eggs. Conservation projects gradually helped ospreys return to Scotland. Today several pairs of ospreys nest in the Tweed **valley** every year.

This osprey has plucked a fish out of the River Tweed.

The River Tweed meets the sea at the border town of Berwick-upon-Tweed.

From the 1100s to the 1400s, the border between Scotland and England was moved several times. Berwick-upon-Tweed was sometimes in Scotland and sometimes in England! Today it is England's most northerly town.

Other UK rivers

The River Wye flows along the border of Wales and England. Wildlife includes bats and the rare polecat!

The River Clyde was important for shipbuilding in the 1900s. Shipbuilding was once a major industry in **Glasgow**.

The Great Ouse hosted the Oxford and Cambridge boat race in 1944. This is the only time the race has not been held on the Thames.

The River Bann is the longest river in Northern Ireland. It flows into Lough Neagh, which is the largest lake in the United Kingdom.

The Clifton Suspension Bridge crosses the Bristol Avon's dramatic cliffs and **gorge**.

The River Tyne flows into the North Sea after a journey of 100 km (62 miles) across northern England. The city of Newcastle upon Tyne is famous for its swing bridge.

Location of rivers

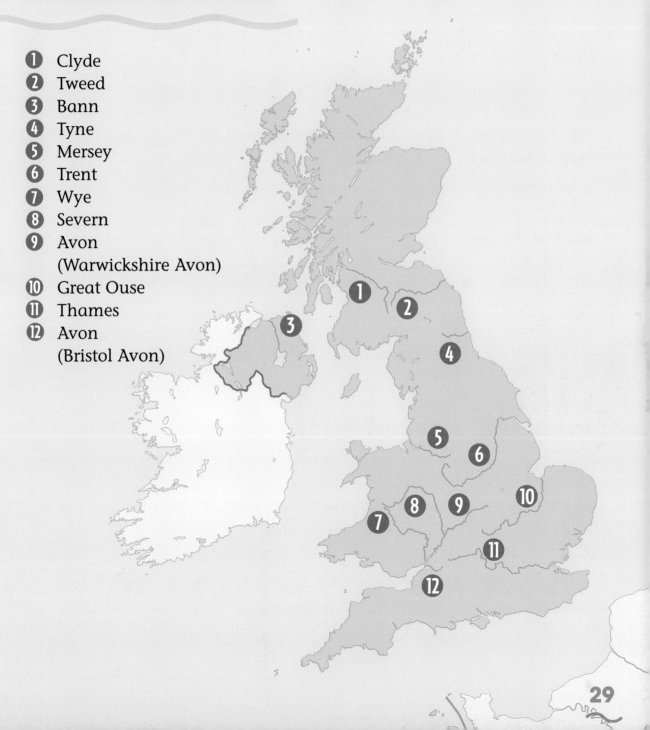

1. Clyde
2. Tweed
3. Bann
4. Tyne
5. Mersey
6. Trent
7. Wye
8. Severn
9. Avon (Warwickshire Avon)
10. Great Ouse
11. Thames
12. Avon (Bristol Avon)

Glossary

burn Scottish word for a stream

canal human-made waterway linking rivers

capital city the main city of a country

estuary the mouth of a large river where it meets the sea

ferry a small boat or ship that takes passengers across a river

generator a machine that produces electricity

gorge a deep, narrow valley with steep, rocky sides

habitat the place where an animal or plant lives

Industrial Revolution a period in history when many factories were built and people moved from the countryside to work in towns and cities

lock an enclosed chamber on a river or canal, with gates at either end, to raise or lower boats from one water level to another

medieval a period in history, sometimes known as the Middle Ages, from around 500 to 1500 CE.

pollution anything that is harmful or poisonous to the environment

port a town or city with a harbour for ships to load and unload

source where something begins

spring a place where water flows up out of the ground

stream a small, narrow river that often feeds into a larger river

tide the rise and fall of water in the sea every day

trade buying and selling things

tributary a smaller river or stream that flows into a bigger river

turbine a machine with blades that turn round

valley an area of low ground between hills or mountains

Find out more

Books

Rivers (Kingfisher Readers), Claire Llewellyn (Kingfisher, 2013)

Rivers and Lakes (Amazing Habitats), Leon Gray (Franklin Watts, 2015)

Thames (River Adventures), Paul Manning (Franklin Watts, 2014)

Websites

www.bbc.co.uk/education/topics/zw9k7ty/resources/1
This website has short films giving you a flavour of the UK's rivers.

www.wildlifewatch.org.uk
This website will help you to get involved with helping wildlife, including river wildlife.

Places to visit

Ironbridge Gorge Museums, Ironbridge, Shropshire
www.ironbridge.org.uk
See the historic bridge, discover how to make power from water and step back in time at Blists Hill Victorian Town.

Merseyside Maritime Museum, Liverpool
www.liverpoolmuseums.org.uk/maritime/
Learn about the history of transport on the Mersey.

Thames Barrier Information Centre, Greenwich, London
www.visitlondon.com/things-to-do/place/26941-thames-barrier-information-centre#DxbJtZr8ByCZQ57e.97
Find out more about the Thames Barrier.

Index